Edwards, Doris
North Carolina

CORE LIBRARY OF US STATES

North Carolina

BY DORIS EDWARDS

CONTENT CONSULTANT
Susanna Lee, PhD
Associate Professor
Department of History
North Carolina State University

Core Library
An Imprint of Abdo Publishing
abdobooks.com

abdobooks.com

Published by Abdo Publishing, a division of ABDO, PO Box 398166, Minneapolis, Minnesota 55439. Copyright © 2023 by Abdo Consulting Group, Inc. International copyrights reserved in all countries. No part of this book may be reproduced in any form without written permission from the publisher. Core Library™ is a trademark and logo of Abdo Publishing.

Printed in the United States of America, North Mankato, Minnesota.
052022
092022

THIS BOOK CONTAINS RECYCLED MATERIALS

Cover Photo: Shutterstock Images
Interior Photos: Dave Allen Photography/Shutterstock Images, 4–5; Red Line Editorial, 7 (North Carolina), 7 (USA); ESB Professional/Shutterstock Images, 8–9; J. Carlee Adams/Alamy, 12–13, 43; Geography and Map Division/Library of Congress, 17; Lukasz Stefanski/Shutterstock Images, 19 (flag); Jeff Caverly/Shutterstock Images, 19 (bird); Dorling Kindersley Universal Images Group/Newscom, 19 (dog); Jorge Salcedo/Shutterstock Images, 19 (flower); Simply Photos/Shutterstock Images, 19 (turtle); Farid Sani/Shutterstock Images, 22–23, 45; LM Images/Shutterstock Images, 27; Jeffery Edwards/Shutterstock Images, 28–29; Robert Willett/Raleigh News and Observer/AP Images, 34–35; Skip Foreman/AP Images, 37; Dennis W. Donohue/Shutterstock Images, 40

Editor: Marie Pearson
Series Designer: Joshua Olson

Library of Congress Control Number: 2021951407

Publisher's Cataloging-in-Publication Data

Names: Edwards, Doris, author.
Title: North Carolina / by Doris Edwards
Description: Minneapolis, Minnesota : Abdo Publishing, 2023 | Series: Core library of US states | Includes online resources and index.
Identifiers: ISBN 9781532197741 (lib. bdg.) | ISBN 9781098270506 (ebook)
Subjects: LCSH: U.S. states--Juvenile literature. | Southeastern States--Juvenile literature. | North Carolina--History--Juvenile literature. | Physical geography--United States--Juvenile literature.
Classification: DDC 975.6--dc23

Population demographics broken down by race and ethnicity come from the 2019 census estimate. Population totals come from the 2020 census.

CONTENTS

CHAPTER ONE
The Tar Heel State **4**

CHAPTER TWO
History of North Carolina **12**

CHAPTER THREE
Geography and Climate **22**

CHAPTER FOUR
Resources and Economy **28**

CHAPTER FIVE
People and Places **34**

Important Dates 42

Stop and Think 44

Glossary 46

Online Resources 47

Learn More 47

Index 48

About the Author 48

CHAPTER ONE

THE TAR HEEL STATE

Cars drive slowly on a paved road that winds through mountains. Their passengers admire the views. The license plates show the cars are from states across the country. They are driving the 469-mile (755-km) Blue Ridge Parkway. It connects Great Smoky Mountains National Park in North Carolina to Shenandoah National Park in Virginia.

Some people stop at Linville Gorge along the Blue Ridge Parkway. It's known as the Grand Canyon of the East. A series of

The Blue Ridge Parkway has many scenic views.

waterfalls here drops 90 feet (27 m). Other cars travel to the banks of the New River in the northwestern corner of the state. It is thought to be the oldest river in North America.

THE BILTMORE ESTATE

One of North Carolina's top places to visit is the Biltmore mansion in Asheville. It's the largest building that was once a private home in the United States. The massive house sits on 8,000 acres (3,237 ha) of land. It has 65 fireplaces, 43 bathrooms, and 35 bedrooms. Built in 1895, the Biltmore was home to the wealthy Vanderbilt family. Today it is a popular tourist attraction and employs 2,400 workers. There are restaurants, a winery, shops, gardens, and miles of hiking trails on the property.

ABOUT NORTH CAROLINA

North Carolina is part of the southeastern United States. The eastern side of the state meets the Atlantic Ocean. To the west is Tennessee. Georgia and South Carolina are to the south. Virginia forms the state's northern border.

North Carolina has several

MAP OF NORTH CAROLINA

Take a look at this map. How does it help you better understand the locations discussed in Chapter One?

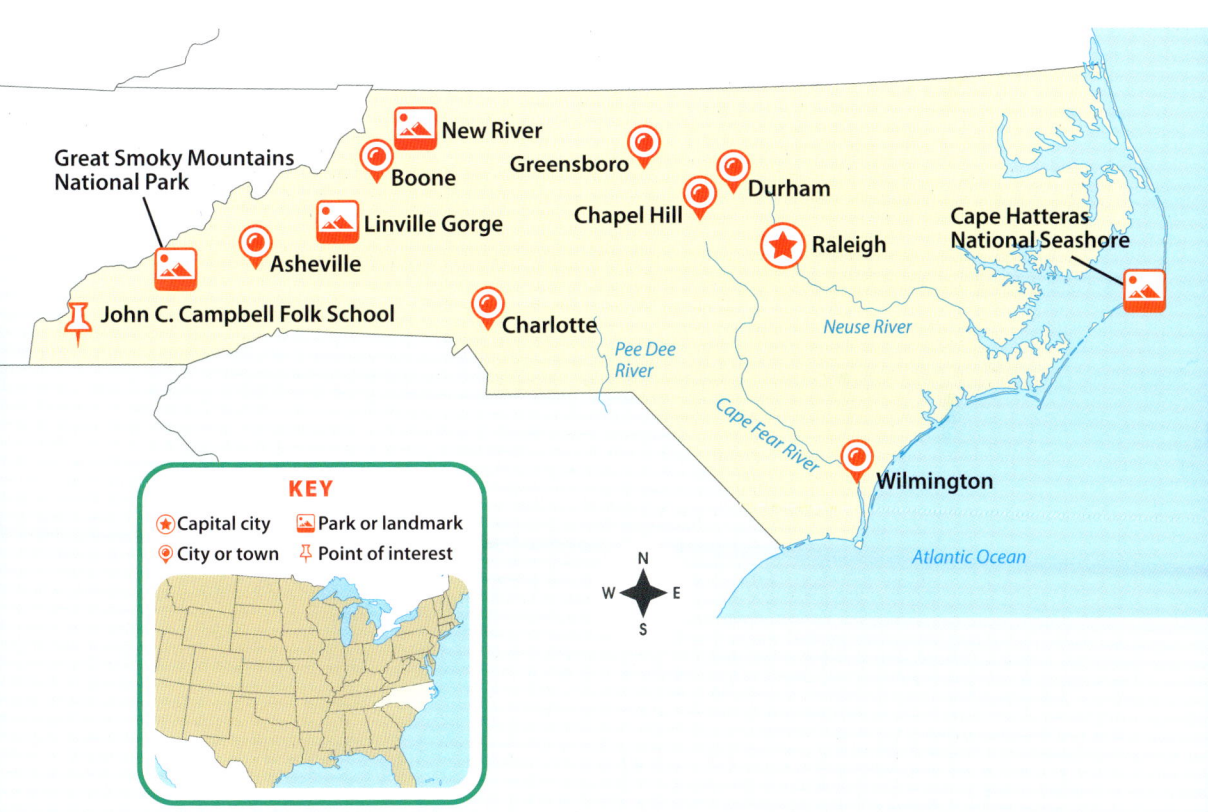

Raleigh and its suburbs make up one of the fastest-growing metropolitan areas in the nation.

different regions. Each one provides resources for people, plants, and animals. The Appalachian Mountains run through the western part of the state. Many small towns are located in this area. Larger towns in the mountains include Asheville and Boone.

Central North Carolina is called the Piedmont region. It is more urban. It has large cities, such as Charlotte and Greensboro. Raleigh, the state capital, is

located there too. Many large colleges are in this area, including Duke University in Durham and the University of North Carolina at Chapel Hill. Researchers and scientists work at the colleges. The colleges are also the homes of well-loved sports teams.

The coast has fewer cities than the middle of the state. Here, Wilmington and other coastal towns sometimes experience strong storms, such

PERSPECTIVES

THE WORLD'S FIRST FLIGHT

The Wright Brothers National Memorial is located at Kill Devil Hills in the Outer Banks. The museum honors Orville and Wilbur Wright. These brothers from Ohio made history there on December 17, 1903, when they made what may have been the world's first successful powered flight. They chose the area because of wind, sand, and isolation. Ashley, a ranger at the Wright Brothers National Memorial, explained, "The wind is to help create enough lift that's needed to get their gliders into the air. The sand is for soft landings, sometimes crashes, when things don't go as well, and the lack of people or isolation is so they won't have to worry about people stealing their ideas."

as hurricanes. But the coasts have many things to offer visitors. Cape Hatteras National Seashore was the United States' first coastal preservation area. This scenic region is part of a group of barrier islands called the Outer Banks. They border the Atlantic Ocean. Here visitors can tour the Bodie Island Light Station, the Cape Hatteras Light Station, and the Wright Brothers National Memorial.

North Carolina has a rich history. American Indians have called the area home for thousands of years. It was one of the first 13 colonies settled by the British. Its nickname, the Tar Heel State, is also part of the state's history. In the 1700s people who lived there used boiled tar from pine trees to seal ships. Workers often went barefoot in the summer. Their feet collected tar. This may be the source of the nickname. North Carolina continues to make history today. From scientists to sports stars, artists, and more, many people are proud to live within the state's borders.

EXPLORE ONLINE

Chapter One discusses the Blue Ridge Parkway. The article at the website below goes into more depth on this topic. Does the article answer any questions you had about the road's history and famous destinations?

AMERICA'S HISTORIC DRIVE

abdocorelibrary.com/north-carolina

CHAPTER TWO

HISTORY OF NORTH CAROLINA

North Carolina was home to several American Indian nations long before Europeans arrived. Each nation lived in different parts of the state. The Cherokee people have lived near the mountains for approximately 12,000 years. The Tuscarora lived in central North Carolina. They farmed corn. Algonquin peoples lived in the northeast along the Outer Banks. They relied on fishing and hunting. Near the southeastern coast were the Waccamaw Siouan people. They traveled

People can learn about the history of the Cherokee at the Museum of the Cherokee Indian in North Carolina.

PERSPECTIVES

THE CHEROKEE NATION

In the 1700s the Cherokee Nation was the largest of all the southern American Indian nations. It had approximately 25,000 members. Its territory reached from the Ohio River to present-day Alabama. When European settlers arrived, they took the Cherokee lands. In the 1800s, the Eastern Band of Cherokee Indians bought back 57,000 acres (23,000 ha). Today many members still live there. It is called the Qualla Boundary. Annette Saunooke Clapsaddle is among them. She published a novel in 2020 about being Cherokee. She said, "My Cherokee ancestors have been here, we would say, since the beginning of time."

along the Neuse, Pee Dee, and Waccamaw Rivers during different seasons.

SETTLERS

English explorer Sir Walter Raleigh started one of the first European settlements in what is now North Carolina on Roanoke Island in 1587. This settlement is called the Lost Colony because it disappeared with little trace. Today the state's capital city is named after Raleigh.

After Europeans first arrived in the area, they traded goods with American Indians. As more and more Europeans immigrated, they took over the American Indian peoples' hunting and fishing grounds. In the 1700s, wars broke out between American Indians and white people over control of the land. White settlers enslaved Black and American Indian people to plant and harvest tobacco and work in the timber industry. Slavery was key to North Carolina's economy.

> ## GEORGE MOSES HORTON
>
> George Moses Horton was a Black man. He was born into slavery. Horton taught himself to read as a child while enslaved. Then he started reciting poems at markets. From there, Horton made his own poems. In 1829 he published his first book of poems. Horton was the first Black man to publish a book in the South. His poems talked about his childhood. They also protested slavery.

At this time, North Carolina was part of the original 13 American colonies. But many colonists wanted to be free from British rule. The Revolutionary War (1775–1783) began over this wish for independence.

On July 4, 1776, the representatives of the 13 colonies adopted the Declaration of Independence. In it they declared independence from England and created the United States of America. That same year, North Carolina wrote its first state constitution. During the war, five major battles were fought in North Carolina. The last was the Battle of Guilford Courthouse on March 15, 1781. This battle is seen as a turning point of the war because many British troops were either killed, wounded, or captured. On November 21, 1789, after the war was over, North Carolina ratified the Constitution and officially became the twelfth US state.

1800s

The US government passed the Indian Removal Act in 1830. As a result, many American Indians in North Carolina and nearby states were forced onto crowded reservations. The US Army removed more than

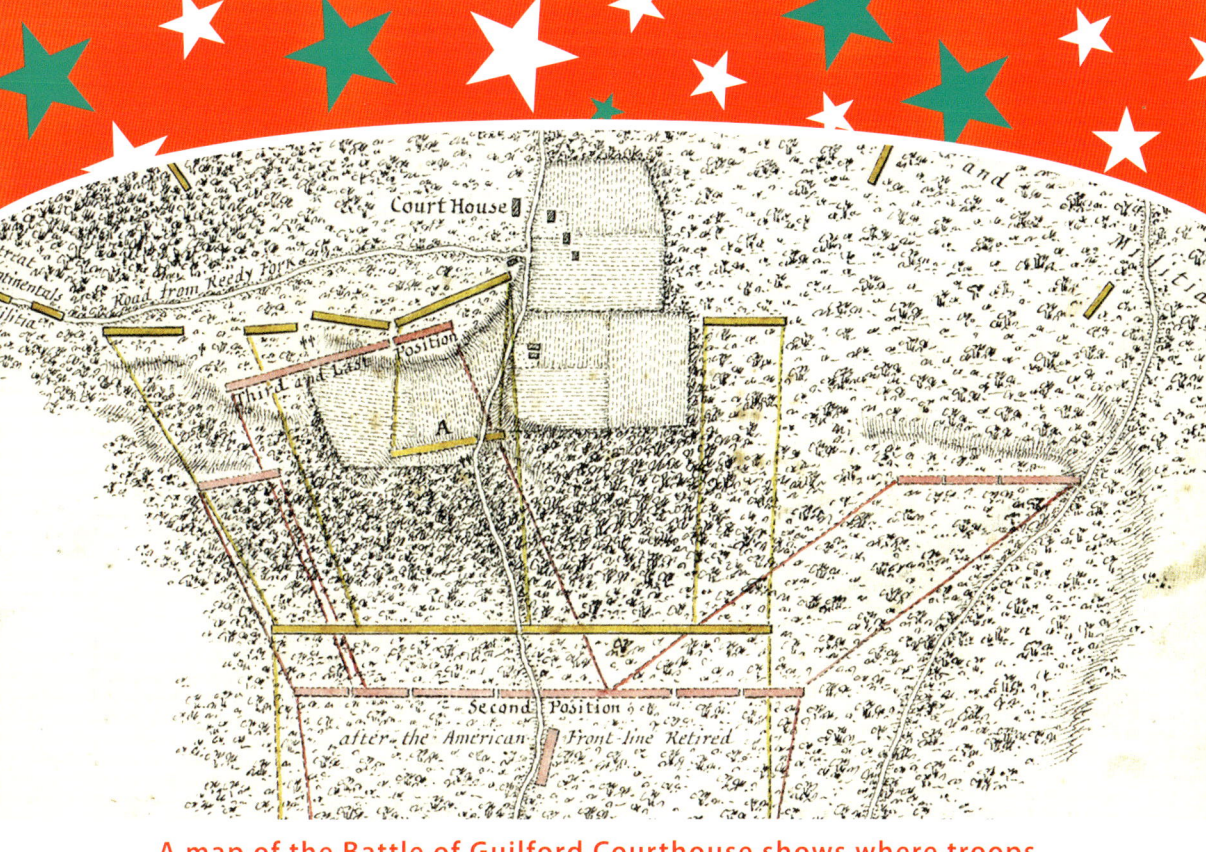

A map of the Battle of Guilford Courthouse shows where troops fought within the location.

15,000 Cherokee people from their homes in North Carolina, Georgia, Alabama, and Tennessee in 1838. The people had to walk 1,000 miles (1,600 km) to what is now Oklahoma. The brutal journey was later named the Trail of Tears. More than 4,000 Cherokee died. But a small group escaped the march. They stayed in the North Carolina mountains. This group became the Eastern Band of Cherokee Indians, which still lives there today along with other American Indians.

By the mid-1800s, many southern states believed slavery should be legal in US territories. Northern states disagreed. As a result, 11 southern states, including North Carolina, seceded from the United States in 1860 and 1861. These states created the Confederate States of America. This action led to the Civil War (1861–1865). Some North Carolinians supported the Union, and others supported the Confederacy. North Carolina rejoined the United States after the Confederacy's defeat.

After the Civil War, Confederate states had to reintegrate. The process was difficult. New laws in North Carolina called Black Codes made it legal for white people to continue racial discrimination. Black Codes kept Black people from holding certain types of jobs and made it difficult to quit a job. But new federal laws and constitutional amendments from 1867 to 1870 helped change things for a time.

NORTH CAROLINA
QUICK FACTS

Examine these facts about North Carolina and its state symbols. How do they help you better understand the state?

Abbreviation: NC
Nickname: The Tar Heel State
Motto: *Esse quam videri* (To be rather than to seem)
Date of statehood: November 21, 1789
Capital: Raleigh
Population: 10,439,388
Area: 53,819 square miles (139,391 sq km)

STATE SYMBOLS

State bird
Northern cardinal

State flower
Dogwood

State dog
Plott hound

State reptile
Eastern box turtle

CIVIL RIGHTS ERA

Still, issues of racism continued in North Carolina. Jim Crow laws allowed Black people and other people of color to be treated as inferior. The laws required people of color to use separate bathrooms, go to different schools, and sit in certain areas in theaters and on buses. North Carolina created restrictions on voting, such as poll taxes and literacy tests. These made it harder for people of color to vote.

Many people of color in North Carolina and other states fought for their rights during the civil rights movement. In 1960 four Black students staged a sit-in at a segregated Woolworth's lunch counter in Greensboro. They refused to leave. News of this nonviolent protest spread across the country. It helped convince politicians to change racist laws.

STATE GOVERNMENT

Today North Carolina has three branches in its state government. They are the legislative, judicial, and executive branches. The legislative branch consists of elected officials who create, change, and vote on new and existing laws. This branch is separated into two groups, the Senate and the House of Representatives. Bills passed in the legislative branch go to the executive branch. Here the governor can sign bills into law. The last is the judicial branch. It includes the courts of North Carolina.

FURTHER EVIDENCE

Chapter Two discusses the growth of slavery in North Carolina in the 1700s and 1800s. Identify one of the author's main points. What evidence does the author provide to support this point? The website at the link below also discusses the topic. Find a quote on this website that supports the author's main point. Does it offer a new piece of evidence?

COLONIAL LEGACIES
abdocorelibrary.com/north-carolina

CHAPTER
THREE

GEOGRAPHY AND CLIMATE

North Carolina has three main regions. The Coastal Plain is closest to the Atlantic Ocean. The Piedmont is in the middle of the state. The Mountains region covers western North Carolina. Each region has unique weather.

The Coastal Plain is swampy and flat near the ocean. It was the first region to be settled by Europeans. Ships could easily deliver and pick up goods on shore. The soil farther inland is rich for crops and perfect for farming.

North Carolina is fairly flat along the coasts.

PERSPECTIVES

ONE OF THE BEST PLACES TO LIVE

For residents and visitors, North Carolina is a wonderful state to discover. The state is filled with art and culture. It has 41 state parks, ten national parks, and four national forests. Many people find the weather comfortable too. Writer and North Carolina expert Harry Hoover says, "While summers can be hot and humid, winters are extremely mild in North Carolina—a pleasant surprise for most residents moving in from out of state. Between the Outer Banks, Lake Norman, the US National Whitewater Center and the Great Smoky Mountains, residents will never run out of places to explore."

In the center of the state, rolling hills make up the Piedmont. Scientists believe these hills may be the remains of an ancient string of mountains. Today forests cover the hills. This region also has many rivers, including the Cape Fear. The rivers flow toward the coast.

Western North Carolina is mountainous. The Appalachian Mountains extend south to north. This mountain range is made up of several groups of mountains. In North Carolina, these groups include the Great Smoky Mountains and the Blue Ridge Mountains. Mount Mitchell is part of the Black Mountains. It is the highest peak east of the Mississippi River.

VARIED WEATHER

Each region of North Carolina has unique weather. The southeastern part of the state is considered subtropical. Summers are long, hot, and humid. But near the coast, the ocean keeps temperatures warmer in the winter and cooler in the summer.

The western mountains have cooler temperatures than the coastal areas. These mountains keep cold air from traveling eastward. The Coastal Plain is more likely to experience the effects of hurricanes. As climate change increases weather extremes, North Carolina's coastal region is at greater risk of flooding.

PLANTS AND ANIMALS

With so many types of landscapes and weather patterns, plants and animals have adapted to the state's regions. Pine and hardwood trees grow in the forests of the Piedmont and the Appalachians. Tropical plants and flowers such as the azalea thrive in the southeast.

PITCHER PLANTS

The green pitcher plant thrives in North Carolina. It lives in habitats with a lot of moisture. Pitcher plants are different from most plants. They don't get nutrients from soil. Instead, they eat insects. The pitcher plant forms a tall vaselike leaf. Inside is a sweet, sticky liquid. Insects are attracted to the liquid. They fall into the plant and can't get out. The pitcher plant gets most of its nutrients from the trapped insects.

The blossom of the dogwood tree is North Carolina's state flower. Three species of dogwood grow throughout the state. The alternate-leaf dogwood is common in the mountains. The gray dogwood grows in the mountains of northwestern North Carolina.

Ospreys feed on fish.

The flowering dogwood lives in deciduous forests all over the state.

Flying squirrels live in North Carolina's forests. The cape-like skin between their limbs stretches to help them glide from tree to tree. Eastern box turtles are found throughout the state. These brightly colored reptiles can live to be 30 years old. On the coast, people can watch ospreys dive. They use their long talons to grab prey from the ocean. Cardinals, which are the state bird, sing and soar throughout North Carolina's cities and suburbs.

CHAPTER FOUR

RESOURCES AND ECONOMY

North Carolina is full of natural resources. The Coastal Plain has rich soil. Farms in this region grow most of the nation's sweet potatoes. They also raise pigs and poultry.

Almost 60 percent of North Carolina is covered in forests. Many people in the Piedmont and mountain regions work in forestry. Companies cut down trees to use for paper pulp. Some of the wood is also used to make furniture.

North Carolina is home to several paper mills, including this one in Canton.

HIGH POINT

The city of High Point looks much like other cities. With 114,059 people, it's the ninth-largest city in the state. But twice a year, High Point nearly doubles in size. More than 80,000 people flock to the High Point Furniture Market each fall and spring. The fair is the largest furniture show in the world. It has more than 12 million square feet (1.1 million sq m) of display space. Shoppers can buy carpets, handmade beds and dressers, and more.

The Appalachian Mountains contain coal deposits that formed over millions of years. Coal can be mined and then burned in order to make electricity. Coal power plants were a big industry in North Carolina beginning in the 1850s. But people began to realize that burning coal is bad for the environment. The process increases carbon dioxide levels in the air, which traps heat and contributes to climate change. Beginning in the 2000s, the demand for coal dropped. This led to plans to shut down many of the plants.

Other sources of energy began to replace coal. Natural gas travels in pipelines directly to homes and businesses. Solar power and hydroelectricity became popular industries in North Carolina too. In 2019 North Carolina ranked second in the nation in solar energy production.

BOOMING BUSINESS

North Carolina has lower taxes than many other states. This has encouraged large companies to come to the state. More than 300 of these companies set up offices in an area known as the Research Triangle.

The Research Triangle is located in the cities of Raleigh, Chapel Hill, and Durham. Each of these cities also has a major university. Companies there are leaders in science, technology, engineering, and math (STEM) research. In 2020 a virus began to spread in the country. It caused a disease called COVID-19. Researchers in the Triangle were hard at work. At the University of North Carolina, scientists created tests, vaccines, and treatments for COVID-19. In 2021 Google and Apple announced they planned to open campuses in

PERSPECTIVES
WOMEN IN STEM

Software engineer Phoebe T. Thermitus works at Lenovo, a technology company in the Research Triangle. Thermitus helps create diverse and inclusive communities at the company. Dr. Nan Jokerst is an associate dean at the Pratt School of Engineering at Duke University. She is also cochair of the Triangle Women in STEM board. "The opportunities for women in STEM are absolutely fantastic, and intentionally creating an environment where women can thrive in these fields is tremendously exciting," Jokerst said in an interview.

the Triangle. These moves would create thousands of new jobs.

In addition to science and research, North Carolina is home to a booming entertainment industry. The state's varied landscapes and mild weather are selling points for film and television production companies. Many movies and shows have been filmed in Charlotte. Some of the most famous are the movie *The Hunger Games* and the TV series *Homeland*.

STRAIGHT TO THE
SOURCE

One travel blogger wrote about why North Carolina is a great place to visit:

> North Carolina is one of those lucky states with a great diversity of climate to enjoy from the ever-popular coastal plains to the spectacular Great Smoky Mountains which show us the rainforest side of things. . . .
>
> The North Carolina Mountains and the Asheville area are known for natural beauty, art and crafts and an abundance of farms, farmers' markets, tailgate markets, and restaurants that offer a wide array of unique and local edibles. . . . There is an endless variety of places you can see and explore in the North Carolina area.
>
> Source: "10 Best Things to Do in North Carolina, USA." *Two Monkeys Travel Group*, 15 Apr. 2019, twomonkeystravelgroup.com. Accessed 15 Oct. 2021.

BACK IT UP

The author of this passage is using evidence to support a point. Write a paragraph describing the point the author is making. Then write down two or three pieces of evidence the author uses to make the point.

CHAPTER
FIVE

PEOPLE AND PLACES

Many famous people throughout history hail from North Carolina. A lot of them are musicians. Some well-known singers include blues singer Nina Simone, jazz musician John Coltrane, and hip-hop artist 9th Wonder.

Basketball players Michael Jordan and Stephen Curry both grew up in North Carolina. Author Harriet Jacobs and social justice activist Ella May Wiggins were from the state too. Writer and poet Maya Angelou also lived in North Carolina for many years, though she

Michael Jordan, *left*, entered the Basketball Hall of Fame in 2009.

PERSPECTIVES

WALKER CALHOUN

The music of the Cherokee people includes many types of instruments. Traditionally flutes, drums, and rattles were common. Today guitars, fiddles, and mandolins are often used. Cherokee Walker Calhoun lived in North Carolina until his death in 2012. He became famous for singing Cherokee songs and strumming the banjo. Calhoun received an award from the National Endowment for the Arts in 1992. He explained how he learned to play the banjo. He said, "I would often sneak down one of the banjos and play it, and I would put it back before my brothers got home."

wasn't born there. She taught at Wake Forest University in Winston-Salem.

POPULATION

North Carolina has a long history of European settlement. As a result, 62.6 percent of the people who live there are white people who are not Hispanic or Latino. Nearly 10 percent of the state's population is Hispanic or Latino. About 3 percent of the state's population is Asian.

The Woolworth's lunch counter is part of the Civil Rights Trail, which includes locations across many states.

Around 22 percent of North Carolina residents are Black. Some of these people descended from enslaved people. Racism has persisted throughout North Carolina's history and into the present day. Visitors to North Carolina can learn more about civil rights and the US civil rights movement. The International Civil Rights Center and Museum is located in Greensboro.

It is housed in the same building where the famous Woolworth's lunch counter sit-in took place.

Today about 1.6 percent of North Carolinians are either American Indian or Alaska Native. The state is home to the largest population of American Indians east of the Mississippi River. The Lumbee Tribe of North Carolina is based in the southeast. The Eastern Band of Cherokee Indians in the west has federal recognition. Visitors to the town of Cherokee can learn about the area's history at the Museum of the Cherokee Indian.

SPORTS AND CULTURE

For sports fans, North Carolina universities are known for their basketball programs. Duke is famous for its men's and women's college basketball teams. The men's team plays in the historic Cameron Indoor Stadium. The state also has several pro sports teams. Fans cheer on the Charlotte Hornets in basketball, the Carolina Panthers in football, and the Carolina Hurricanes in hockey. The University of North Carolina's teams are called the Tar Heels after the state's nickname. Its teams include football, baseball, and men's and women's basketball.

The John C. Campbell Folk School in Brasstown is the nation's oldest school dedicated to folk crafts. It started in 1925. The school offers year-round classes for adults in crafts, art, music, dance, cooking, gardening, nature studies, photography, and writing.

Many people flock to North Carolina simply for its natural beauty. The state is home to nearly 96 miles (154 km) of the famous Appalachian Trail,

BILLIE RUTH SUDDUTH

North Carolina has a rich history of crafts. People there historically made cloth, baskets, and many other items. Billie Ruth Sudduth is one of many artists who continues the tradition today. She handweaves reed baskets. Sudduth uses natural dyes. Today her baskets can be found in art museums throughout the United States. She also teaches others how to weave baskets.

North Carolina's wild horses descend from captive horses that were shipwrecked or abandoned on the Outer Banks.

which stretches from Georgia to Maine. Those seeking beaches and ocean waves can visit Cape Hatteras National Seashore on the coast. Wild horses roam the northernmost beaches of the Outer Banks. The horses' heritage in the area dates back more than 500 years. No matter what people are interested in, they'll find many adventures and attractions in the Tar Heel State.

STRAIGHT TO THE
SOURCE

A big part of North Carolina's appeal is its art scene and culture. The North Carolina Arts Council helps arts organizations and artists thrive. In March 2020 a flyer about the arts in the state read:

> *For 50 years, the North Carolina Arts Council has invested in artists and arts organizations to create a strong arts infrastructure that reaches every corner of our state. We know that you believe, as we do, that the arts make North Carolina a great state to live and work.*
>
> Source: "Why the Arts Matter in North Carolina." *Americans for the Arts Action Fund*, 20 Mar. 2020, artsactionfund.org. PDF. Accessed 24 June 2021.

CONSIDER YOUR AUDIENCE

Adapt this passage for a different audience, such as your principal or friends. Write a blog post conveying this same information for the new audience. How does your post differ from the original text and why?

IMPORTANT DATES

10,000 BCE
Cherokee people live in the mountains of modern-day North Carolina.

Mid-1500s
Spanish explorers are the first Europeans to see what is now North Carolina.

1776
North Carolina representatives write the first state constitution.

1789
North Carolina becomes the twelfth US state.

1861–1865
North Carolina and the other states that seceded from the United States fight for the Confederacy in the Civil War.

1903
Orville and Wilbur Wright make the world's first powered flight at Kill Devil Hills.

1960
The Greensboro sit-ins begin in order to protest segregation.

2020
Scientists in the Research Triangle create new tests and treatments for COVID-19.

STOP AND THINK

Tell the Tale

Chapter One describes visiting the Blue Ridge Parkway. Imagine you are driving along this road. What do you see? What do you find the most spectacular about the experience? Write 200 words explaining your experience.

Dig Deeper

After reading this book, what questions do you still have about American Indians in North Carolina? With an adult's help, find a few reliable sources that can help you answer your questions. Write a paragraph about what you learned.

Why Do I Care?

Maybe you aren't interested in learning about different industries. But that doesn't mean you can't think about how natural resources, such as those found in North Carolina, affect your life. Think about some of the resources mentioned in Chapter Four. How would your life be different if you didn't have access to those resources?

Take a Stand

Some people in North Carolina live in big cities. Others live in rural areas. How are rural areas and cities different? Do you prefer living in a big city or a small town? Why?

GLOSSARY

adapt
to change over time to develop a feature or skill that helps an animal or plant survive

civil rights
rights that people have for personal freedom

climate change
a human-caused global crisis involving long-term changes in Earth's temperature and weather patterns

constitution
a document laying out the basic beliefs and laws of a nation or state

economy
a place's system of goods, services, money, and jobs

nutrient
a substance that humans, animals, and plants need to stay strong and healthy

ratify
to sign or give formal consent to an agreement or document

secede
to leave a political union

ONLINE RESOURCES

To learn more about North Carolina, visit our free resource websites below.

Visit **abdocorelibrary.com** or scan this QR code for free Common Core resources for teachers and students, including vetted activities, multimedia, and booklinks, for deeper subject comprehension.

Visit **abdobooklinks.com** or scan this QR code for free additional online weblinks for further learning. These links are routinely monitored and updated to provide the most current information available.

LEARN MORE

Johnson, Anna Maria. *North Carolina*. Cavendish Square, 2019.

Smith, Sherri L. *What Is the Civil Rights Movement?* Penguin, 2020.

Stanborough, Rebecca. *Exploring the South*. Abdo, 2018.

INDEX

American Indians, 11, 13–17, 36, 38
Angelou, Maya, 35–36
Appalachian Mountains, 8, 24, 26, 30, 39

Biltmore Estate, 6
Blue Ridge Parkway, 5–6, 11

Calhoun, Walker, 36
Charlotte, 7, 8, 32, 38
civil rights, 20, 37–38
coal, 30
Coastal Plain, 23, 25, 29, 33

dogwood, 19, 26–27

farming, 13, 23, 29, 33
forests, 24, 26–27, 29, 33

High Point, 30
Horton, George Moses, 15

Outer Banks, 10, 13, 24, 40

Piedmont, 8, 23–24, 26, 29
pitcher plant, 26

racism, 18–20, 37–38
Raleigh, 7, 8, 14, 19, 31
Research Triangle, 31–32
Revolutionary War, 16
rivers, 6, 7, 14, 24–25, 38

settlers, 11, 14–15, 23
slavery, 15, 18, 37
sports, 9, 11, 35, 38–39
Sudduth, Billie Ruth, 39

weather, 24, 25–26
Wright Brothers, 10

About the Author

Doris Edwards lives in Portland, Oregon. She has written many books for young readers. When she isn't writing, you can find her gardening or baking tasty cookies for her grandkids.